Pain, love

Arabella Skye

India | USA | UK

Pain, love and loss © 2024 Arabella Skye

All rights reserved.

No part of this publication may be reproduced, stored in a retrieval system, or transmitted, in any form or by any means, electronic, mechanical, photocopying, recording or otherwise, without the prior written permission of the presenters.

Arabella Skye asserts the moral right to be identified as author of this work.

Presentation by *BookLeaf Publishing*

Web: www.bookleafpub.com

E-mail: info@bookleafpub.com

ISBN:9789358314892

First edition 2024

DEDICATION

To my girls, Cici, Molly and Lillibelle, I love you.

To Maggie and all my family and friends that's supported me this year

ACKNOWLEDGEMENT

to all of those who have been there for me this year, you'll know if the shoe fits.

I'm fine

I'll tell you I'm fine,
but the light has gone from my eyes,
sometimes I feel numb,
no energy to run,
that's unlucky to me, not some
the pain inside feels like a tonne

Sometimes I feel sad,
it hurts so bad
all I feel is pain
my tears, they fall like rain
I'll tell you I'm fine,
I'll pretend this time

Sometimes it's the anger
I want to hurt them
like a rose thorn stem
but I hurt myself instead
on glass shards I will tread
It's okay.. I'm fine
don't cross the line

Honestly it's the pain
it always ends the same
a cut here, some pills there

another suicide 'scare'
It's okay, I'm fine
when I die a star I'll shine

Happiness what is that?
enjoy life at the drop of a hat?
go back to the old me
the faker you want to see?
I'm good at that shit,
fake it just a little bit
don't tell anyone at all
they don't want that call

it's okay, smile it's fine
i'll succeed some time.

Grieve

I always think of you
I miss you it's true
every single day I feel blue
not seeing you

I miss the school runs
and all the fun
the watching TV and cuddles
the hot chocolate and winter snuggles

Singing and dancing to our favourite song
like nothing could go wrong
..but it did
now this pain and sorrow I cannot rid

I need to let go
but the sorrow will always show
I don't know how
to let you go now

they say I need to grieve
and it is something i do believe
but it's hard when you're still around
knowing your safe and sound

Girls

I loved you yesterday
I love you now
I always have
I always will

When they took you
my heart broke in two
full of sadness and regret
it felt like my life was set

misery and pain
no sunshine just rain
letting everyone down
like a closed down town

It hurts so much
not allowed to feel your touch
missing your cuddles
and jumping in puddles
doing lots of art
going to the park

Watching you giggle
whilst we danced and wiggle
picking you up from school

going to the swimming pool

Snuggles under the blanket watching TV
throwing stones into the sea
geocaching by the tree
having fun, now that's key

I hope you know what you mean to me
even if no-one else could see
I wanted to give you what I never had
I never wanted you to feel bad

Just happy and proud
with love around
a mum full of pride
I honestly tried

I'm sorry I failed
I know I let the ship sail

no more reading you story tales
or tucking you in at night
none of that is fair or right
I hope the stars shine bright

And you sleep well tonight
I know you'll be alright
I just wish it was with me
I will always love you, you see

AMHT

I wish I could tell you what's in my head
but it's an out of control story to be read
I want to run, scream and shout
get on any transport that's about

Disappear without a trace
end this life long race
they say that it gets better
they even put it in the letters

we can't help you is what they say
you have to help you, it's the only part to play
but truth be told I would if I knew
I don't know how to that is true

Guidance, support, help is what I need
then I'll grow from that seed
instead I feel lost, alone, a burden to all
the pain, the sorrow, fear stands tall

other people tell them how you help them lots
I feel like I'm left to rot
I know I have to help myself
but there's no book upon that shelf

To guide me along the way
that's why I need your support
but all you seem to say
is do it yourself, then your help you abort

Am I not worthy of your time?
will I ever begin to shine?
a future I cannot see,
happy I'll never be.

Me

Have you ever looked in the mirror
and hated what you see?
hated the woman you've always been?
hated the person that is yourself

longed to be like the girls in the books on the shelf
felt like a burden to everyone around
failing each time you make a sound
wishing you could have done better

I just want to be happy not some trend setter
I don't know what I want to be
it's hard when a future isn't something you see
I hate everything about me
I wish I could change me with a key

But truth be told I was never alright
just a messed up sight
I've tried to run away at night
when they try and save me I put up a fight

I know you're all fed up of me
I'm fed up of me too can't you see?
but I can't escape being me

on the run I will forever be

Drink

Sometimes I drink to forget
but it always ends up in regret
I just long to forget you, just for a little bit
just so the pain of losing you, elsewhere will sit

But truth me told I lose all control
I end up in a deeper darker hole
I'll try and run away
I won't get caught I'll pray

Hurt myself, end it all
then someone see's and makes the call
they come and lock me away
but my minds lead me astray

Then along comes the shame
it really is always the same
nothing takes the pain away
it just seems to always stay

So then I'll go all withdrawn
wishing I was never born
keep it all inside

Until I drink again..

Lilly

Your little smile
made everything worthwhile
your giggle filled me with pride
especially the 'pick you up and swing ride'

Picking you up after school
teaching you to swim in the pool
stranger danger, crossing the road
you even learnt hygiene, with me you learnt a load

I showed you patience and love
at Harriers you soared high like a dove
soon you called me mummy
and my life felt so warm and sunny

Your smile used to beam
when we all took Ted to the stream
running up Bankside playing tag
putting together your Tinkerbelle bag

When it was thunder and lightening you come for hugs
sat playing games on the road rug
you and Molly rolling down the hill

that memory makes me smile still

Baking cupcakes with icing on your nose
on a hot day, a water fight with the hose
tucking you in at night
hiding by the door as you get back up, I always
caught you bang to rights!

Pink this, unicorn that
watching teen titans on the TV you'd be sat
doing your hair, pretty each day
'my mummy did it' to everyone you'd say

Mummy's big Minnie goes everywhere you go
that teddy shows I'm always there you know
you brought so much joy into my life
losing you cut me like a knife

I miss you so
I hope you know
I hope you're happy in your new home
I hope it's a home full of love your shown

Wish

They say to wish upon a star
your dreams coming true won't be far
or blow out your birthday candle
it will come true, just patience to handle

Make a wish, break a wish bone
with upon a skipping stone
drop a coin in a wishing well
or even cast a wishing spell

Truth be told I tried them all
it doesn't work, I still had the call
when will my life finally go right
I'm sick of putting up a fight

now all I wish for is to forget
my life is so full of regret
I got what I wanted for it all to go
now sadness is all that I sow

Molly

When I first met you, you was so shy
I'm so proud of how your confidence has grown
It makes me happy cry
my heart melts at your smile and giggle
the more you was with me I saw it more, little by little

Every time I would poke your nose
you'd pretend to bite and my smile arose
going to the park when you needed a chat
singing Yungblud loudly on the roundabout we'd be sat

Taking you to your first ever concert
we dance and sand really taking part
Yungblud aiming his drink like a dart
taking selfies on our phone
you always changing my ring tone

You stealing the spoon while I try and cook
over my shoulder at my phone you'd look
you was always so nosey it would make me laugh
annoying all the Morrisons staff

going round all the shops
trying on all the tops
stealing from my hand my food and drink
laughing as you did it, your confidence grew I think
making our own slime
playing all the time

collecting all the David Walliams books
watching a new programme together we'd both get hooked

messing around acting silly
being a fantastic older sister to Lilly
just me being your mum
meant an absolute tonne

you are my pride and joy,
I will love you until the end of time

Mind

Sometimes life feels really hard
each day, each memory is tarred
it's really hard knowing where to turn
when most places would watch you burn

But there is one place I feel really safe
on the phone, in group or face to face
the staff are kind and caring
it's a place that's okay for sharing

I feel like they understand
some may even get it first hand
staff and service users feel like family
staff put on groups happily

At safe haven we get distracted
with others we've interacted
in groups we make friends
arts and crafts, we make things it depends

art group and women's group is fun
I feel better even on the days I feel done
sometimes I come to group feeling blue
but I always walk out happier it is true

We're so lucky to have Mind
it's a charity that should be full of pride
such a difference it makes
to people just like me
after all still here I wouldn't be

if I didn't have the people of Mind

Christmas

Christmas time for some is full of fun
but for some the magic hurts a tonne
this season used to make me happy
now the memories hurt and I get snappy

Matching pyjamas and Christmas eve boxes
peanut butter on bread for the foxes
sat together watching Christmas films on TV
watching Santa go by on his sleigh, is now just a dream

Listening to music while we done the tree
it all meant so much to me
now without you, Christmas cheer is hard to see
without you, hurt is all I'll be

Christmas day will be hardest of all
not watching you opening your gifts
not even a call
all 3 of you in different places, apart
we should be together from the start

Now my Christmas spirit is gone
no more singing Christmas songs
no more Christmas selfies on my phone

No more hiding things in ice and chipping away
like a stone

I never knew the true meaning of Christmas
until I had you
now there's no white Christmas, only blue

Cici

You think my love for you is dead
but the more I don't see you it grows instead
our relationship was great at the start
then you met him and we started to part

All I wanted was to protect you
I did and still love you it's true
I wish you had given me a chance
to be the mum you deserved at last

You're beautiful, bright and strong
everything that's happened to you, was wrong
I wish I protected you so much
but instead our lives will not touch

I'm sorry I didn't know how to be a mum
it's just something I had never done
I tried so hard, the whole thing was tarred

I miss watching K dramas with you
or you teaching me about k-pop over a brew
our midnight nuggies when you was feeling sad
I was there each time you felt bad
even sat outside the school toilets talking you out

when he made you want to shout

I hope your happy where you are
you really are such a star
you can do anything you put your mind too
I know you won't believe it but it's true

I am and always will be proud of you
I'll always love you sweetheart, that's true

Social

No matter how hard I try
I'm under a microscope they will pry
they say if I work hard on my mental health
my contact will increase, the happier i'll be

But how am I supposed to trust
any social worker, when I was treated like dust
on phone calls I would wait and wait
for him to not show he made me irate

my contact cancelled all the time
how am I supposed to shine?
I begged and begged for help from you
I was let down you know it's true

I was thrown in the deep end
but those kids became my godsend
then all that happened and you took them away
but I hoped they was happy where you placed
them, at least I prayed

Now I'm getting worse and worse
I feel like I was used and it hurts
you had nowhere to place them so you gave
them to me

not to help but watch me fail you see

But truth be told I never regret
taking them in, it showed me happiness I was set
losing them broke me beyond repair
my heart is so broken, on my sleeve I wear

I tried my best it just wasn't enough
they and I had been through some bad stuff
if you had given me the support
maybe my girls I would have had at the end of court

now I'm just sad and all alone
cant even call them properly on the phone
instead I have no rights as a step-mum
now my trust in everyone is so done

Him

I thought you was the one
I thought having you I'd finally won
but I was just too naive to see
no-one would want to be with me

I was just easy for you
I did everything you asked me too
paid for everything, including your debt
part of me wishes that you, I'd never met

I will always be grateful for the girls
with them I won a world full of pearls
they're the only good thing you ever gave me
because honestly you broke me you see

So I'm stuck between a rock and a hard place
at one point you made my heart race
now it's broken in two
never again call me your 'boo'

All you wanted was sex and a slave
now looking back I feel used and abused
looking back at our selfies you never smiled
like having me around was just effort you piled

Things got worse after the kids came
all you wanted was to play on your game
everything was left to me
the sole parent I would simply be

It was worth it for their smile I would see
but all you would do was moan about all three
your life had changed you wanted it back
but how you couldn't want them my brain would rack

Now you pretend to be the doting dad
The one I wanted when we had them so bad
did I deserve all this I ask?
did I do something wrong to fail the task?

Now I'm more miserable than before
sat here on a cold hard floor
wondering why..it's me again?

Maybe

I wonder what it would be like
to stop everything and go on strike
to disappear or become someone else
would I be happy or would I still be sad?

Fed up and so depressed
struggling to get up and get dressed
would I have a decent job
instead of sitting in my room alone to sob

Maybe I won't be all alone
with family and friends all around
I'll feel like a queen upon her throne
maybe I won't scrimp for my last pound

Maybe I'll have my own home
and travel to places like Rome
maybe people would want me around
instead of being the rebound

People wouldn't be fed up of me
maybe the real me somewhere we will finally
see
maybe I'll be happy
instead of grumpy and snappy

Maybe I'll be a good mum
always positive and full of fun
instead of losing them and doing it wrong
maybe I haven't been good enough all along

what if I was really pretty
instead of looking like miss piggy
I'd be able to look in the mirror
instead of it being another trigger

I know I can't be someone else
I know I can't go on strike
Maybe my only chance is to disappear at last

Mask

People wonder how I seem so fine
but truth is I mask all the time
out with family or a friend?
put the mask on until the end

When you get home
your emotions will free roam
you will feel like a burden
like your lonely all of a sudden

The negative thoughts will close in
like someone has taken the lid off a tin
they didn't want to be with you
how could anyone like you, you fool

you spent all that money?
those debts are getting worse honey!
you don't deserve to be happy
now you start to feel crappy

Your in that cycle now
your in your head having a row
hurt yourself, kill yourself..no!
ha!, you're not stronger than your mind, tell it so!

It doesn't matter your head will win
the suicidal behaviour will begin
the mask came off now you have no energy to fight
stop trying to fight you don't have the right

you're worthless pathetic a burden to all
do the right thing, on a bridge you'd stand tall
if you jump you may paralyse yourself
then more of a strain on society you will be

Something that will definitely work is more key
maybe more pills just don't tell anyone you see

By now you've been stopped your energy levels have dropped
your asleep in a psych ward bed
they'll release you again

until next time you let the mask come off

You

When I first met you I felt so low
So I just want you to know
those sessions made me feel so safe
although we was working on my emotions

I learnt how to smile
and that felt great
it put my mind in a better state
you helped me see things

you helped me cut the strings
you made me feel strong
like I hadn't done anything wrong
eventually when my relationship was over

And I was scared I wouldn't cope
you helped me stay and passed me the rope
I clung on tight but you had to go
And then it got harder, I told you so

You had such a warm heart and smile
you even helped with the trial
you made me feel like I could do anything
like I had something for the world to bring

You showed me what safe felt like
when it felt like learning to ride a bike
you showed me what a good relationship was
you saw my flaws

You had a job to do
but I am so grateful to have met you

Sleep

Imagine trying to sleep
but your so scared you start to weep
you grip hold of your teddy so tight
but nothing can make it right

You feel like someone is watching you
you swear you can see them too
you get up and turn on the light
but your rooms empty nothing in sight

it feels so real, you check the door
it's locked still so you pace the floor
you turn off the light get back into bed
but it's there again, long black coat, eyes red

you put your glow in the dark stickers on the wall
but the lights off, he stands tall
some say psychosis but they don't care
another symptom of trauma it's not rare

so close your eyes tight
lets hope he don't bite

Goodbye

Would you miss me if I was gone?
would you ask what went wrong?
but every picture she's so happy!
her confidence grew she became sassy!

she was going out more,
less isolated, less of a bore
she became less snappy
more laughter more happy

it seemed she had her life on track
she became a better liar
she hid it so well
no-one could tell

this whole time she was planning her final
goodbye

Milton Keynes UK
Ingram Content Group UK Ltd.
UKHW051256220624
444380UK00018B/663